Kitty Cat Plays Inside

Story by Annette Smith   **Illustrations by Ben Spiby**

Kitty Cat liked playing inside on cold days.

She played by the big chair.

Look at Kitty Cat!
Look at the big chair!

"No, Kitty Cat.

Come away!

Come away!"

Kitty Cat played in the basket.

She played in the wool.

"Meow! Meow! Meow!

I can not get out,"

said Kitty Cat.

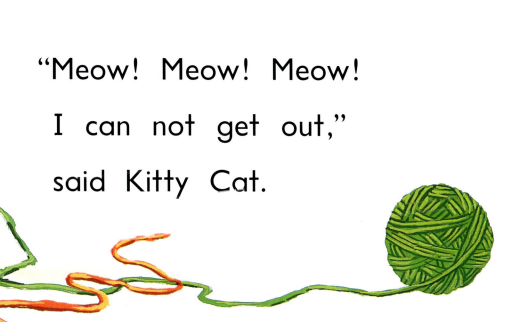

"Kitty Cat!

You are a naughty little cat.

Stay out of the basket."

Kitty Cat ran up the curtains.
She looked down.

"Meow! I'm way up here,"
said Kitty Cat.

"Come down here.

Come down!

You are a naughty little cat.

You can go outside!"

Kitty Cat looked outside.
Fat Cat looked back at her.

"Meow," said Kitty Cat.
"I can see Fat Cat.
I am not going outside."

"I will stay inside,"
said Kitty Cat.
"I am a good little cat."